SAWNEY BEAN

Like all great myths, this beauti[ful play, though] based on the true story of an eigh[teenth century] cannibal, touches the reader's p[syche and appeals] to his deepest needs for artistic e[xperiences that] are essentially timeless: the sem[i-historical setting] creates a poignant image of innoc[ence through his] loyal wife, Lila, whom he finally s[acrifices]; Jot and Rain, who represent different elements of nature: and Solomon, Sawney's spiritual son, who eventually develops a will of his own.

The play works on many levels and gives birth to many complex themes: poetically and imaginatively it examines the nature of innocence and knowledge, it poses questions about the meaning of religion and arising from this it has a strong, driving ritualistic form and flow that grips the reader entirely. Above all, it is theatrically and drama--tically exciting - as the successful Traverse Theatre Club production showed, it communicates an intense fervour that sweeps both audience and reader along in its wake.

Robert Nye is already well-known as a novelist and poet, whose poems have been frequently broadcast by the B.B.C. His collection of poems, DARKER ENDS, has been published by Calder & Boyars in their 'Signature' series and was praised by Tribune as 'exceptionally beautiful, truthful': and his short stories, TALES I TOLD MY MOTHER, also published by Calder & Boyars, received general acclaim. But it was his exciting first novel, DOUBTFIRE, that really put him on the literary map, receiving such accolades as 'funny, savage, witty', from the 'New Statesman' and 'breathless, brilliant' from the 'Guardian' for its study of adolescence. SAWNEY BEAN is his first published play.

Bill Watson is Literary and Features Editor of 'The Scots--man' and in 1969 won a Scottish Arts Council Literary Award for his first novel BETTER THAN ONE. Reviewing the book in 'The Spectator', Barry Cole said, '.....he uses words as though the whole concept of language were an invention of his own, and one he is confident of patenting.'

PLAYSCRIPT 36
'sawney bean'

robert nye &
bill watson

CALDER AND BOYARS · LONDON

First published in Great Britain 1970
by Calder & Boyars Limited
18 Brewer Street, London W1R 4AS

© Robert Nye, Bill Watson 1970

All performing rights in these plays
are strictly reserved and application
for performances should be made to
C & B (Theatre) Ltd.,
18 Brewer Street, London W1R 4AS

No performance of these plays may be
given unless a licence has been obtained
prior to rehearsal.

ALL RIGHTS RESERVED

Printed in Great Britain by
The Pitman Press,
Bath, Somerset

SAWNEY BEAN was first presented by the Traverse Theatre Club during the Edinburgh Festival of 1969, with the following cast:

SAWNEY	Colin McCormack
LILA	Sue Lefton
SOLOMON	Toby Salaman
JOT	Anthony Haygarth
RAIN	Ann Russell
SHEPHERD	Sue Carpenter

The play was directed by Max Stafford-Clark.

SAWNEY BEAN

CHARACTERS

SAWNEY

LILA

SOLOMON

JOT

RAIN

SHEPHERD

ACT ONE

Scene One

(It is black. Pool of light grows on the floor. Pause. Into the pool as from a height springs the figure of SAWNEY BEAN. He is a long man, his arms are long, his hands have a big spread and tend to live a little away from his body. The way he carries himself is unusual: at first he seems loose-limbed, a gangling man, but on acquaintance you perceive that he is articulate with his body - it is just that he has no self-consciousness in the sense that he is not affected by the eyes of others. Where the light is the stage is deep in sand - this is the seashore, part sand part rock. On the other side of the stage is the entrance to his cave, still in the blackness and unseen by the audience. He has landed in a crouching position. Pause. Slowly he extends his right leg and settles onto his left buttock with his left ankle under his right knee, and leans forward and strokes the sand with the back of his left hand. When he strokes the sand he is caressing something that is a friend, a mystery and perhaps an enemy. This stops. He sits back leaning on his hands and looks straight across the stage into the dark. Leans on one hand, listens with his eyes, starts pointing by flicking forefinger of other hand out from the thumb with a distinct chafing sound.)

SAWNEY:
Who? (This is not really spoken interrogatively, but speculatively and levelly.) Who? In the dark in front of me, in the sun behind me. Who would do that? How would he do that? My ears would hear him - they hear the sand move and a bird run into the water. They would hear. They don't tell me to say "Who?" I see other men first; they don't see me. Who? Who? Who? (He says this very simply, trying the sound as if that would explain everything.)

9

(He jumps himself together so that he is sitting on his heels and with sudden angry almost punching movements picks up two vast handfuls of sand and crushes them hard together as if he would drive the sand into his skin. Then he puts the edges of his hands together and looks at them and the sand left on them).

SAWNEY:
Who! (Contemptuously). There is nothing, only me, and the sea. And the rock. And the black. And the grass. And fire and stars and shells. And crabs and birds and seaweed. And the tree with all its leaves which are kind to me. And the rain, I like the rain. (Lights out. Blackness).

(Lights. SAWNEY and LILA are sitting on the rocks outside the cave. LILA is combing her hair).

SAWNEY:
You could make up people.

LILA:
Mm?

SAWNEY:
You could, you could make up people.

LILA:
Then so could you.

(Pause).

LILA:
Why should it be me?

SAWNEY:
You can make things. I've seen you.

LILA:
What things?

SAWNEY:
The seagull. The seal. The crab.

LILA:
    I didn't make them, Sawney. I mended them.

SAWNEY:
    No, you made them. They came down broken and you
    made them. A broken crab is not a crab. Other crabs
    know that... they all fall on it and eat it up.

LILA:
    It's still not true to say I made it. It was there first.

SAWNEY:
    You could make up people.

LILA:
    Well if you want people go and sit in a tree and watch
    till somebody comes.

SAWNEY:
    I don't want people to eat. I want people to be with.
    People you and I can share.

LILA:
    Sawney love, I can't make people.

SAWNEY:
    Now you try. You try and think how to make people.

LILA:
    Well. I could get some bits of stick, and some grass.
    And some clay. And some feathers. And seaweed. And
    shells to make eyes.

SAWNEY:
    That would only remind me of people.

LILA:
    I could teach a bird to talk.

SAWNEY:
    A bird talks already. You could teach the tree to talk.

LILA:
    I don't need to. Haven't I sat in that tree and haven't

11

I listened to it talking to me?

SAWNEY:
Is that true?

LILA:
It said it was tired.

SAWNEY:
That would be true.

LILA:
It said it knew a creature once who killed a man.

SAWNEY:
I don't want a dead man.

LILA:
Then it knew a man. A tall man. With black hair. Who laughed.

SAWNEY:
How old?

LILA:
Oh young. He never walked. He always ran, or jumped.

SAWNEY:
Why?

LILA:
Because he was young. The tree said the creature said the man said where do I come from?

SAWNEY:
Where did he come from?

LILA:
Me. I made you a man.

SAWNEY:
You made me a man. I knew you could. When will I see him?

LILA:
   You won't see him unless you look for him.

SAWNEY:
   Where?

LILA:
   Where I looked. I made you a man; you make more of him.

SAWNEY:
   (He is eager, she is pleased that he is eager - that is the feeling of this scene): How do you do it?

LILA:
   What colour are his eyes?

SAWNEY:
   I don't know. (Seeing them). Blue, blue.

   (She smiles, and lets him get on with it).

   He has blue eyes. He has long arms, and sometimes he walks on his hands.

LILA:
   No, Sawney (laughing).

SAWNEY:
   Yes he does. (Puts the heels of his hands over his eyes). Look, you can see him walking on his hands. Go on, look.

LILA:
   (Also putting her hands over her eyes): Yes, I can see him. Oops, he's fallen down.

SAWNEY:
   So he has.

   (They both fall into laughter).

LILA:
   That was funny.

SAWNEY:
   It was funny. It was different.

LILA:
   It felt strange.

SAWNEY:
   I liked it, but it hurt me somewhere. (Pause). It was like a loss.

LILA:
   You still have your eyes, love.

SAWNEY:
   That's true.

LILA:
   You didn't fall down.

SAWNEY:
   That's true.

LILA:
   But it did hurt. I wonder what it was.

SAWNEY:
   (Throws out an arm): Something went out there. It's like the white spray that's made between the sea and the rocks.

LILA:
   Tell me.

SAWNEY:
   The sea hits the rock and the white spray breaks off it (pause while he works it out). So the sea has wasted some of itself, and that hurts.

LILA:
   The white spray is lovely, Sawney.

SAWNEY:
   That's true. (Long pause). I'll want something to do

tomorrow.

LILA:
You can make me a new comb.

SAWNEY:
Then we'll go along the edge of the sea in the morning till we find a strong white bone, and in the afternoon I'll work it for you.

LILA:
That's good.

SAWNEY:
And sometime we'll make the man again.

LILA:
Yes, Sawney.

Scene Two

(The girl RAIN, and the boys JOT and SOLOMON are sitting on the rocks.)

RAIN:
(Laughs).

(Pause).

JOT:
Why did you laugh?

(RAIN laughs more quietly).

RAIN:
Nothing.

SOLOMON:
You don't laugh at nothing.

RAIN:
I do. You know I do.

SOLOMON:
Yes, but what was this nothing?

RAIN:
I won't tell you, Solomon.

JOT:
I asked you first.

RAIN:
Ask me again then.

JOT:
> Why did you laugh, Rain?

RAIN:
> I thought how funny it would be...

JOT:
> Yes?

RAIN:
> (laughing). Well, it would just be very funny.

SOLOMON:
> What?

RAIN:
> If I was paddling in the sea one night and the sea froze and I was just standing there for ever and ever until it melted. (Laughs).

JOT:
> You mean you'd just be standing up there? Stuck? With your feet on the ground, and the ice round your ankles? While we were up here, sleeping away in the cave and sitting round the fire, and you'd be stuck out there... you'd be covered with snow. You'd get more and more snowy. Oooh. We'd throw snowballs at you.

RAIN:
> So you would.

(She collapses with laughter. JOT also collapses).

SOLOMON:
> So we would.

(SOLOMON also collapses. They simmer down).

JOT:
> I don't like it when the sea freezes.

SOLOMON:
> Why?

JOT:
    (Stands up, mildly agitated): Because...

SOLOMON:
    Say why.

JOT:
    I'm trying to. It's because he stops talking to us. That's one thing. He goes away from us, and when he comes back he stands and looks at us from the back of his eyes.

SOLOMON:
    Is that all that worries you?

JOT:
    No, but it's all I remember.

SOLOMON:
    I remember something else.

JOT:
    What then?

SOLOMON:
    When the sea freezes he goes and walks on it, for days. I've watched him wandering in long straight lines, until he was so far out that he was a speck, and then he was nothing, and as he went away he got slower... and slower... and I've never seen him look back when he goes out there. He goes quite alone and we wait on the shore.

RAIN:
    There's something else.

SOLOMON:
    Yes, what? (Knowing the answer).

RAIN:
    When he comes back, he brings nothing with him.

SOLOMON:
    That's what I mean.

JOT:
>That's what I don't like. He brings something back but I can't see it. When he goes anywhere else he always brings something we can see, or taste, or touch: something to use... like today, he's gone to get this comb for Lila. But when he's been out there he just comes back and starts looking at us, as if we were someone else... as if we were different.

RAIN:
>It's as if he goes out there and finds something, and then forgets it, forgets what it was, and has to keep going back.

JOT:
>But why does he look at us like that?

SOLOMON:
>I don't care how he looks at us. I want to know why he goes out there, I want to know who he meets.

RAIN:
>He doesn't meet anyone.

SOLOMON:
>He meets something; something that makes him afraid.

JOT:
>Perhaps the sea won't freeze this year.

SOLOMON:
>It's going to freeze all right, and you won't have to wait long either.

RAIN:
>What are you going to do, Solomon?

>(SOLOMON says nothing, and he and RAIN look at each other).

JOT:
>If you go after him, Solomon, he'll break your neck. Anyway, they'll be back soon. There's still some of that leg left, it's nice and lean, he likes it lean. You'd

better get it ready, Rain. They'll be hungry when they come back.

(RAIN finishes looking at SOLOMON, and exits).

SOLOMON:
They're not just looking for a comb you know.

JOT:
Mmmm?

SOLOMON:
It's you. They're going to give you a name soon.

JOT:
Today?

SOLOMON:
I think so. Rain thinks so too.

JOT:
Why does he have to give us names?

SOLOMON:
Don't you want to have a name then?

JOT:
I don't mind; but why does he do it?

SOLOMON:
He likes naming things. He gives everything a name. But you're right... I wonder why. He was the first of us, so perhaps it made him less alone to look at the sea and call it Sea, and to touch the rock and say Rock, and suck the air and say Air. Perhaps he spoke to them.

JOT:
Perhaps they spoke to him.

SOLOMON:
I don't think so.

JOT:
Perhaps they asked for names.

SOLOMON:
    Have you asked him for a name?

JOT:
    I don't know any.

SOLOMON:
    Well think for yourself how he does it.

JOT:
    I don't know how he does it.

SOLOMON:
    You might find you do if you think about it.

JOT:
    (Stares into space, concentrates). It's not good. I can't.

SOLOMON:
    Think like this. You are alone here, you have always been alone here, you've never spoken to anybody else, and no one has ever spoken to you... What would you do?

JOT:
    I'd laugh. Because there would be no one to see.

SOLOMON:
    Why? Would you be happy?

JOT:
    No. But I'd laugh. (Pause) And then I'd listen. I'd hear the tide running into the cave and the cry of the wind. I'd hear my heart. I'd hear a bird shift in the air, and leaves hit the ground, and the flames talking in the fire. (Listens to the flames a bit in his mind).

SOLOMON:
    Well?

JOT:
    Well.

SOLOMON:
   Well, you'd want to give them names.

JOT:
   (Still abstracted): Give what names?

SOLOMON:
   All these birds and leaves and flames and things.

JOT:
   No, I don't think so. No, I don't think I would. I mean, it would be too soon. It would always be too soon. I think it's too soon to give me a name. I don't think I want a name at all. I won't use it.

SOLOMON:
   It's not you who'll be using it. We'll be using it about you.

JOT:
   I don't care. I'll give myself a new name every day.

SOLOMON:
   You won't know who you are.

JOT:
   That would trouble you, wouldn't it, not to know who you are. Strange things trouble you. You ask strange questions. And you want answers.

SOLOMON:
   Answers. Names are answers.

JOT:
   They're not very good answers.

SOLOMON:
   Not to you perhaps. They seem to serve him in some way. How?

JOT:
   Perhaps they helped him to remember.

SOLOMON:
    What's he got to remember? He was the first of us. No. I think it's something else. I think he wanted to frighten someone.

JOT:
    Who?

SOLOMON:
    Someone who's not here yet.

JOT:
    No one's coming. No one comes here except the ones he catches. He doesn't need to frighten them.

SOLOMON:
    No. It's not one of them. And it's not one of us either.

JOT:
    Maybe it's himself.

SOLOMON:
    Himself?

JOT:
    Maybe he wants to frighten himself.

SOLOMON:
    But I told you: it's someone who's not here yet.

JOT:
    He's not here yet now, is he?

SOLOMON:
    But he's coming.

JOT:
    That's it.

SOLOMON:
    What's it?

JOT:
    When he comes, what?

SOLOMON:
   I'll see him.

JOT:
   That's it. You'll see Sawney Bean. But he was the first of us. You never saw him then. Before he had a name.

SOLOMON:
   Well?

JOT:
   Well, maybe there was more. Some more that he didn't give the name to.

SOLOMON:
   More? More of <u>him</u>? More of Sawney Bean? More? There can't be <u>more</u>!

JOT:
   Wait.

SOLOMON:
   Wait?

JOT:
   Wait.

   (Enter Rain).

RAIN:
   Lila's coming. He's not with her.

JOT:
   How's she walking?

RAIN:
   She's combing her hair.

JOT:
   That's good.

   (Enter LILA, quietly happy. Goes over to SOLOMON and

holds his head in both hands, looks at him and greets
them all saying: "Children!" Goes over to JOT on her
way to RAIN, caresses him in passing and kisses RAIN.
These greetings are sensual but not explicitly sexual).

LILA:
Sawney's gone into the land. (She moves, arms half up
and out-stretched in a kind of magic semi-circle of an
arc, back and forward; she is describing a ritual dance
which the children understand, it has a loping rhythmic
gait. We shall shortly see SAWNEY executing this dance
as he mesmerises one of his victims). He's gone into
the land.

RAIN:
(Laughing with pure pleasure): Does he know or is he
looking?

LILA:
He'll bring something back. It was a long way up the
shore. I had found the bone and he had made my comb
for me and had loved me, and after the rain... you
had the rain?... he went up onto the grass and stretch-
ed, and suddenly I saw him putting his head down to the
earth and listening, and he waved and went off among
the trees.

SOLOMON:
He likes catching them in the trees.

RAIN:
Of course he likes catching them in the trees. He can
slide from tree to tree hiding (acts all this out). And
they never see him. He sees them a long way off between
the branches and follows them. And when he knows where
they are going he passes (whispers this) silent and
out of sight high over their heads and drops down a tree
where they will come and waits (a few steps of the
ritual dance) and... catches them!

JOT:
That was good, Rain, I liked that. I felt it.

LILA:
> I think she's been there. I think she's caught one herself and never told us.

RAIN:
> Shshsh! (Turning away the idea). Of course I haven't!

LILA:
> Of course you haven't. I liked how you told it, that's all.

SOLOMON:
> Don't you want to?

RAIN:
> No I don't want to. It's his work. He does it for us.

LILA:
> Why, do you want to do it, Solomon?

SOLOMON:
> No, I don't want to do that. I don't want to catch food. I don't want to hide in trees and bounce around in them like a squirrel. I'd dig traps and let them fall in, onto sharp sticks, so that they'd be there when I wanted them. Like a spider making webs and collecting flies in its own time. Then I'd be free to do what I wanted. Can I see your new comb, Lila?

LILA:
> (Looking at him). Yes. Have it.

SOLOMON:
> (Taking the comb). He makes good combs. Come here, Rain. (Takes Rain's arm and sits her down. Combs and strokes her hair). How would you catch them, brother?

JOT:
> I would empty your traps, brother.

SOLOMON:
> You shouldn't empty my traps. You should think up something for yourself.

JOT:
>Oh, I would be thinking about something else.

SOLOMON:
>What would you be thinking about?

JOT:
>How not to fall into your traps.

LILA:
>You talk about it. He does it. Come with me, Rain, give her the comb, Solomon.

>(Exit RAIN and LILA).

JOT:
>Rain doesn't like when you talk like that.

SOLOMON:
>No one does. Does it matter?

JOT:
>If she told Sawney he would be angry.

SOLOMON:
>She won't tell Sawney.

JOT:
>Lila might.

SOLOMON:
>Lila won't.

>(End of scene. Fade)

Scene Three

(In the forest. The setting sun spies a SHEPHERD. Above him SAWNEY waits).

SHEPHERD:
I hate sheep. Silly things. What's not wool might as well be. Off all over the place with never a backward glance. That's four this year I've lost, and now I'm lost myself. No one comes here, there are no paths. This place is very still; even the wind does not come so far. I must find a place to sleep. God be kind to me when night comes, and safety last till morning.

(Sits down and takes off his boots, and rubs his feet, whistling).

SAWNEY:
(Dropping lightly to the ground, watches the shepherd, himself unnoticed for a moment. He has a leaf in one hand and compares the leaf and the palm of the other hand. He stands for a moment doing this, then squats on the balls of his feet before the shepherd, and hands him the leaf, which the shepherd takes, his surprise is so great). My hand: look. It has marks on it like the leaf. I saw this just now while I was waiting.

SHEPHERD:
(He is in shock and therefore behaves reasonably; probably he knows he is going to be eaten, but refuses to realise this and so falls in with Sawney's way, not ingratiatingly but because it confines him safely to the moment and engages his mind). Are you shipwrecked?

SAWNEY:
No. Look, look at the leaf. See. (Traces leaf-lines on

his hand). Two hands together (putting his hands together) makes a leaf. I'm making a leaf. Yesterday we made a man.

SHEPHERD:
Leaves have no fingers.

SAWNEY:
Here, hold your hand up to the sun. (Takes SHEPHERD's hand and holds it up). You can see the blood inside. (Takes the leaf from the shepherd and holds it up). That will be the blood of the tree. (Gives the leaf back to the SHEPHERD).

SHEPHERD:
No. You have it.

SAWNEY:
I don't want to have it. I don't like blood. I like leaves when they're crisp and the blood's gone.

SHEPHERD:
But you have blood.

(SAWNEY sits on a stone.)

SAWNEY:
I have blood. But blood is not strong. It is bone that is good. Bone is hard and simple. When I shut my eyes and sleep at night it is the bone in me that sleeps. The bone is what I am. Blood is not easy. When I sleep it turns into dreams. The blood loves the dark. They join together when I am asleep. They hold each other. They talk. Their talk is like the wind in the trees, it has no words in it. When I wake there is dark mixed in me, because of my blood. Because of my blood there are lies in me. Lies from the dark. Who... tells... the lies. Who tells the lies?

SHEPHERD:
(Speaking with tongues, a litany, but understood, not gabbled). It is a pleasure to stand upon the shore and to see ships tossed upon the sea. It is a pleasure to stand in the window of a castle and to see a battle and

the adventures below. But the best pleasure is to stand
high on the ground of truth and to see the errors and
wanderings and mists and tempests beneath. My mother
taught me that. My father said: The first creature of
God in the works of the days was the light of the sense,
the last was the light of reason. And I have heard that
to say that a man lies is to say that he is brave towards
God and a coward towards men, for a lie faces God and
shrinks from man. This is too much to think. Lies are
a pity. A pity for God, and a pity for me. If men were
sheep they would not know truth or lies. (During this
speech the SHEPHERD has risen and is talking out towards the trees. SAWNEY is behind him, moving backwards and forwards with a creeping gentleness, appalling
and kindly in one so huge, his arms outstretched, his
hands at waist height, in an arc centred on the SHEPHERD,
never coming forward of the SHEPHERD. As the speech
ends he closes in and when the SHEPHERD stops and
lowers his head and as SAWNEY's hands are about to
close around his neck, lights fade out.)

(There is a brief pause of dark. Then lights come up
brilliantly. SAWNEY is standing and the SHEPHERD is
dead).

SAWNEY:
(Stretches, exulting) I live in days and days and days of
sun and light and wind. I live beside the beating sea. I
crunch the sand beneath my feet. I fall upon my Lila on
the grass and smell it sweet beneath me as she moves.
I shout into the wind and make the sea birds fall into the
sky that is always flying. I am Sawney Bean. In the long
days the sun pours heat upon the rock for me to drink
into my bones. I stand against the tide and when it comes
in deep I live within it. I catch the green and wrap it round
my body like a laugh. For me birds fly, for me the
fishes swim, the rock grows hot, the sun has light. I am
Sawney Bean. I am the child of rock and sea and sun, and
made of them. I am Sawney Bean among my days. And
I will last for ever. For ever. He was born and he has
died (lights start to fade). He is stopped. He grows cold.
The flesh will be sour soon and the blood will lose its
salt. Only the bone will keep. He has died. He has

lived. He was born. He is complete. He said God. God he said. They say God. They all say God. He said some words before I broke him: they all say words and all of them say God. God, God, God, God. I would say more than God, God, God. It sounds like a water drop in the cave. I would say more than that. "Lies, lies are a pity." That is true. All lies are one pity. I would say more than that. When I am out on the ice I say more than that. Out on the ice it is quiet. It is quiet here now, and cold and dark, his blood is cold, his bones are cold, the night has come. I will not sleep here. I will talk, I will not let the night sleep. When the sea freezes and is hard and I walk on it I talk then. He talked before I broke him. I will not sleep, I will walk, I will let the dark listen to me. I will let the trees listen and the grass answer and if the wind answers I will listen. If the wind whispers I shall hear. No one listens, no one whispers to me. Out on the ice, when I am there, when I walk on the hard sea, when I talk out on the ice, on the ice, the white ice, in the dark, with the cold, when the blackness reaches from me to the end of the end, I talk, on the ice, I talk... ... ... I talk <u>and he listens</u>. Under the ice he listens, deep down, far down, under the white ice, in the dark, where the water moves he is listening when I talk. He is moving where I move, under me, under my feet, far down, deep down, when I move moving with me, listening. When I do not talk, sometimes when I do not talk, when I stop, when I stand he waits and then he comes close, to me, under my feet, he thuds against the ice and shakes the sea, and if the sea could break ... Who could break the sea, who could break the sea. Who. Who? In the dark in front of me, in the sea beneath me. Who. Not the same. Once at the edge of the ice, once, waiting, but the sun came. Cold, colder, it is cold here (he is crouching down now, touches the shepherd), his bones are growing cold in him. He is meat now. Lies are a pity.

(Cut lights).

(It is early morning. RAIN is listening to the sea in a conch shell. Enter JOT, notices her, stands a moment, himself unseen, puts his two thumbs to his mouth and makes the noise you make with a piece of grass: the call of a sea bird. RAIN registers a little slowly that this has not come from her shell).

RAIN:
    I thought it was the shell.

JOT:
    It was a sea gull.

RAIN:
    It was you.

JOT:
    It was a sea gull. (Jumps down on the beach and joins her). Look, watch this. (Sits beside her).

RAIN:
    What?

JOT:
    Just wait. (Thinks a bit). Now. The sea (makes a movement with his hand to suggest the waves). Your hair.

RAIN:
    What do you mean?

JOT:
    I'll do another one. Four pebbles (lays them out on the beach before her). My knuckles (makes a fist).

RAIN:
    Do another one.

JOT:
    I can't see anything to use.

RAIN:
    Remember something.

JOT:
> That ring of flowers you had on your head that day.

RAIN:
> Oh... ... a snake swallowing its tail!

JOT:
> Good. The mark the tide leaves.

RAIN:
> Yesterday, yesterday!

JOT:
> Yesterday? I hadn't thought like that. I like that. I like yesterday. You can't see yesterday. I was only going to make it something you can see.

RAIN:
> Oh have I spoiled it?

JOT:
> No, you've made it better. You think of one for me.

RAIN:
> What the wind does in a field of grass.

JOT:
> Sorrow.

RAIN:
> Sorrow? I thought it was like laughing.

JOT:
> How strange. When I see the wind moving in the grass it brings me tears, but it makes you happy?

RAIN:
> Grains of sand.

JOT:
> It's an odd difference between two people.

RAIN:
> Grains of sand.

JOT:
>Well, it is odd, Rain.

RAIN:
>Never mind it just now. (Runs some sand through her fingers). Think about grains of sand falling.

JOT:
>The days passing.

RAIN:
>That's good and true.

JOT:
>Well, if that's good and true, what about me being sad and you being happy when the wind blows in a field of grass? Are they both good and true?

RAIN:
>It's all good and true.

JOT:
>You didn't think when you said that.

RAIN:
>No I didn't, but it feels good and true. I don't want to think. We're playing a game. What's it called?

JOT:
>Games don't have names. It doesn't need a name.

RAIN:
>Don't be cross. It's being lovely.

JOT:
>No, I won't be cross. But did you notice that we were being kind with everything, finding a kindness between things, that's what we were doing. And it is a game but we were finding kindness between these things.

RAIN:
>You're making me very fond of you, saying that. (JOT sits down against her knees).

JOT:
    I was in the woods last night. He caught a man.

RAIN:
    You saw him?

JOT:
    I heard him talking. The man was dead. Sawney was afraid.

RAIN:
    Afraid? After the man was dead?

JOT:
    He wasn't afraid of the man. You know that. A man is meat to him, that's all. He was afraid of something under the ice. He was talking on and on about something under the ice. He was remembering. It was as if he was remembering not being alone. Even with us, even with Lila, he's alone... because he was the first of us. But when he goes out there he's not alone. And it's not just something under the ice. It's as if the thing under the ice is the words of whoever he's afraid of knowing.

RAIN:
    Sawney's very big. Not just his body. He's very big.

JOT:
    Then he is afraid because he knows there is something bigger than he is. And it's not only when he goes out on the ice. You see, he was not just remembering. He was talking to it. As if talking would keep it away. As if so long as he was talking he couldn't hear anyone else.

RAIN:
    What did he say?

JOT:
    He said lies are a pity. He said it was quiet out on the ice. He said that when he walked out there he talked. He said it was white and cold and dark. He said the water moved underneath him and the thing moved in the water. He called the thing he. He said that when he stood and waited it came up under his feet and touched the ice

under his feet. It must be like having a shadow that can come and go when it wants to. It was all true, Rain. I knew it was true. It was true, it was true. I ran away. I was afraid, I was afraid I would meet an answer coming towards me as I ran. I slept by the sea, in the soft sand. I felt safe, hearing the sea move. But it will freeze soon.

RAIN:
What does it mean? I think there must be a terrible kindness between him and the thing he is afraid of. It sounds like your game, only not a game. That thing under the ice. And him walking above it. And talking. And being afraid. And wanting to be there, but being afraid, and being Sawney Bean, with <u>anything</u> under his feet. It's as if the snake had swallowed the ring of flowers, and they didn't mind.

JOT:
The sea must be very deep.

RAIN:
And dark.

JOT:
Too deep and dark. Too deep and dark even for Sawney. He likes to see things and give them names. Down there they can have no names.

RAIN:
I think down there there would be just one name. One everything.

JOT:
Or nothing.

RAIN:
Nothing? Alive?

JOT:
Or asleep.

RAIN:
But the thing?

JOT:
    Turned into something.

RAIN:
    Each time the sea freezes.

JOT:
    And each time bigger.

RAIN:
    Did he say that?

JOT:
    No. But he wouldn't go out on the ice unless it was getting bigger. If he keeps going out on the ice it must be getting bigger.

RAIN:
    This is his shore. He does not need the ice. He knows everything here, everything here belongs to him. We belong to him, the rock belongs to him, the sand belongs to him, the cave, the grass, the sky, he gave them all names. He does not need the ice.

    (Enter SAWNEY, carrying a bit of the SHEPHERD wrapped up in a skin. He throws it down).

SAWNEY:
    There's more where that came from. (Turns to JOT). I've got a name for you, boy.

    (Slow fade while they look at him).

ACT TWO

Scene One

(The feast, the dressing-up.)

(For this scene the men will wear: SAWNEY, scatterings of soldiers' outfits, sumptuous but tatterdemalion, a strange helmet and a big battle-axe; SOLOMON, a particoloured jester's tunic and wild hairy breeks with bindings; JOT, a monk's habit with a cowl thrown back and a flag with a big Papal cross on it hanging down from his shoulders at the front. The men will appear shortly, but when the scene opens we discover LILA and RAIN dressing themselves up on one corner of the stage with the meat doing away in a cauldron in another corner. Their style is different; they have seaweed and rowan berries and feathers etc. tied all over their clothes.)

RAIN:
    Jot.

LILA:
    Jot.

RAIN:
    I wonder why he called him Jot.

LILA:
    I wonder why you wonder. I never ask him about names. It seems right to me.

RAIN:
    I like it too, I just wondered. I didn't know he saw him so true.

LILA:
    He sees everything true.

RAIN:
>He does, doesn't he?

LILA:
>He knows these things, he always has.

RAIN:
>Jot is better than Solomon.

LILA:
>Solomon's a good name.

RAIN:
>I don't mean that.

LILA:
>What do you mean?

RAIN:
>I like him better.

LILA:
>I like him better too; but I don't like Solomon less.

RAIN:
>You like Sawney more.
>
>(Enter SAWNEY, strutting rather).

SAWNEY:
>That's a good smell.

RAIN:
>It's not ready yet.

SAWNEY:
>(Sniffing at the pot): Yes it is. (Shouts): Jot! Solomon! (to LILA) I like you like that. (Holds her face in his hands for a second. Turns to RAIN). And Jot will like you like that.

RAIN:
>Jot?

SAWNEY:
>Yes, Jot.

>(Enter JOT, on a laugh).

JOT:
>Look. I'm wearing the sunrise.

SAWNEY:
>Here. Shine on the sea. (He takes RAIN's hand that is furthest away from him in his hand that is furthest away from her, and swings her over at JOT, so that her arm falls around JOT's neck).

>(Enter SOLOMON with his hands behind his back, looking at the sky).

SOLOMON:
>It's going to rain, of course.

LILA:
>(Going to him and drawing him in). Solomon, you must make the first words for the eating.

>(There is a feeling of expectation all round. They seat themselves, man, woman, man, woman, SOLOMON remaining standing).

SOLOMON:
>Who is she the lady-lord,
>At the mouth of the wave?
>Not the swan, not the lark,
>Not the seal of the wave,
>Not the sea-maiden
>Is she.

>(He seats himself. LILA rises).

LILA:
>I bathe my face
>In the nine rays of the sun.
>Honey be in my mouth,
>Affection be in my face,

Love be in the heart of all flesh for me.

(LILA seats herself. JOT rises).

JOT:
    Hey the Gift, ho the Gift,
    Hey the Gift on the living.
    Son the dawn, son of the clouds,
    Son of the sky, son of the star.
    Hey the Gift, ho the Gift,
    Hey the Gift on the living.
    Son of the rain, son of the dew,
    Son of the flame, son of the light.
    Hey the Gift, ho the Gift,
    Hey the Gift on the living.
    Son of the air, son of the sea,
    Son of the moon, son of the sun.
    Hey the Gift, ho the Gift,
    Hey the Gift on the living.

(They all join in the last chorus. JOT seats himself. RAIN rises).

RAIN:
    I went sunways round the tree,
    I cut me a handful of the new grass,
    I dried it gently in the sun,
    I rubbed it sharply from the husk,
    With mine own palms.

(RAIN seats herself. SAWNEY rises).

SAWNEY:
    I heard the sweet voice of the swans
    At the parting of night and day.
    Who should be flying in front?
    The Queen of Luck. The white swan.
    I heard the cuckoo with no food in my belly,
    I heard the dove on top of the tree,
    I heard the screech owl in the night.
    I heard the Queen of Luck, and the bright morning.

(SAWNEY seats himself. By this time they have all

started eating, by taking bits out of the pot with their hands. The rule is that once you have said your say you are allowed to eat. SOLOMON eats wolfishly and SAWNEY, who eats now, with a fastidious elegance. The others just eat. While the eating goes on more sayings are said).

SOLOMON:
    Today is the day of the flesh,
    The snake shall come from the hole,
    I will not touch the snake,
    Nor will the snake touch me.
    The snake will come from the hole
    On the brown day of the flesh,
    Though the snow should be deep
    And the stones lie lost in the ground.

LILA:
    My love he gave to me a knife
    That would cut the soft and hard.
    My love he gave to me a comb
    At the rising of the sun.
    And I promised by the wood
    To meet him in the morning.

SAWNEY:
    In the night we shall have flesh,
    We should have that
    We should have that.
    In this night we shall have songs,
    We should have that
    We should have that.
    Flesh and songs
    We should have that
    We should have that.

SAWNEY:
    (Wiping his mouth on the back of his arm) They all say God when I catch them. I've told you that. But the one who wore this coat (pinches its sleeve) he didn't say God. He stood and made circles in the air with this (touches battle-axe). It shone in the sun. Ah, it was fine.

SOLOMON:
    What did he say?

SAWNEY:
    He shouted 'Come on, then, come on!'

SOLOMON:
    What did you do then?

SAWNEY:
    I threw a rock into his middle. And this (smacks axe again) flew away up into the sun and fell into a tree.

RAIN:
    Tell us how you got Jot's sunrise.

SAWNEY:
    Let me eat, girl.

RAIN:
    You can eat at the same time.

SAWNEY:
    (With his mouth full) I was sitting up in a big tree on the edge of the wood when all these men came along on horses. They were going very slowly. As they came close they made a buzzing sound.

JOT:
    A buzzing sound?

SAWNEY:
    Yes. Like this. (SAWNEY hums in the back of his throat with his mouth open in a very fair imitation of Gregorian chant).

    (They all join in. And laugh. And hum. And laugh. And hum).

SAWNEY:
    Well then, when they came under me I put down my hand and caught this (clutches JOT's flag) one of them was holding it up on the end of a stick. He shouted. And then

they all shouted. And then they all rode off very fast.
But when I pulled this up and then the stick, there he was.

RAIN:
Where?

SAWNEY:
Still holding the stick. I took him off and squeezed his neck.

SOLOMON:
He was very skinny.

LILA:
(Fingering beads about her neck). That's the one who was wearing these.

SOLOMON:
My one made a sound too.

RAIN:
Yes, tell us your story, Solomon.

SOLOMON:
I was asleep in the wood. His noise woke me. He was sitting in a hollow tree, waving his feet, drinking from a little green pot, and sometimes he made a howling sound and talked to himself.

RAIN:
What did he say?

SOLOMON:
He talked about his lady fair.

RAIN:
Lady fair?

SOLOMON
Lady fair. He said she'd told him lies and left him to sleep with the foxes and the wolves. And when he said wolves he suddenly sat up, and dropped his green pot, and his eyes went to and fro, and then he saw me, and

he cried out ooh and he fell over backwards out of the tree and landed on his head. He slept then. I took these clothes off him. He went on talking in his sleep. He didn't say God.

SAWNEY:
He wouldn't say God to you.

SOLOMON:
Why not?

SAWNEY:
Because you weren't going to eat him. They know when you're going to eat them.

SOLOMON:
Oh do they?

SAWNEY:
They know when you're going to eat them.

SOLOMON:
I never thought of this one for eating.

SAWNEY:
You never thought of him at all. You didn't know him. You had no talk with him. Look at you, eating, you had no talk with that. You don't know what you're eating, but I know. I knew this flesh when its tongue still spoke. Its ears heard me speak. Its eyes saw me come. Its nose smelt its own fear. You just eat flesh, Solomon, all of you just eat flesh, but Sawney eats more than that.

JOT:
What do you eat?

RAIN:
You're being unkind.

SAWNEY:
Am I? Being unkind? Do I harm you, Solomon?

SOLOMON:
Would you harm me?

SAWNEY:
　　Could you harm me? (Laughs at the very idea). No, Solomon, I wouldn't harm you. I wouldn't harm a fly.

LILA:
　　Harm.

　　(Silence, because the talk has taken a nasty turn).

JOT:
　　You said "Sawney eats more than that." What does Sawney eat?

SAWNEY:
　　Sawney eats what Sawney knows.

JOT:
　　You talk as if you made them.

SAWNEY:
　　(Piqued): I do make them. I find them. I talk with them. And I catch them. And I feed them to you. I make you. What do you make? (Sits down again and grows calm). Where is my peace going. (Of LILA). She brings me peace. She makes me things. She made me a man, didn't you, Lila. Show these children. Bring him here now.

LILA:
　　A tall man with black hair.

SAWNEY:
　　There was something else.

LILA:
　　A tall man with black hair who laughed.

SAWNEY:
　　How old?

LILA:
　　Oh young. He never walked.

SAWNEY:
> He always ran or jumped. Why was that?

LILA:
> Young, he was young.

SAWNEY:
> (To the others): Can you see him? Jot, can you see him? I can see him. He is walking on his hands.

LILA:
> Has he fallen over?

SAWNEY:
> No, he's sat down. (Smiling). She brings me peace.

RAIN:
> Listen to the sea.

LILA:
> I knew you'd say that.

RAIN:
> How could you know?

LILA:
> I know you.

RAIN:
> (To Jot): Did you know I'd say that?

JOT:
> What?

RAIN:
> About the sea.

JOT:
> No. I knew you were going to say something else. And it wasn't you who was going to say it. It was Solomon.

SOLOMON:
> What was I going to say?

JOT:
> You were going to say: "I can't see him." You were going to put your hand here (shading his brow) and say: "I can't see him."

SOLOMON:
> You mean the man with the dark hair?

JOT:
> Yes. The one who walks on his hands.

SOLOMON:
> I nearly said it. I didn't see him walking on his hands, but I saw him when he sat down. I saw him sitting down when Sawney saw him sitting down.

JOT:
> When you and Sawney saw him sitting down, I saw him rolling about in the grass.

RAIN:
> He was not rolling about in the grass, Jot. He was sitting there, quite still, talking. Talking to you, Lila.

SAWNEY:
> (To LILA): What was he saying?

LILA:
> He didn't talk to me, Rain.

JOT:
> Listen to him now then. Shut your eyes and look.

SOLOMON:
> I see him. He is talking to you, Lila. Listen to him, Lila. He says your hair is very yellow. And your skin is soft and your eyes are cool and kind and when you put your fingers on his face... he is not unhappy.

RAIN:
> Can you hear him Lila? Is he saying that?

JOT:
> Perhaps he's talking to you Rain. Can you see him? I

can't see him now.

RAIN:
No I can't see him. Lila, is Solomon right? Is that what the man's saying?

LILA:
(To the man - she has received SOLOMON's message and wants to let it lie unseen by SAWNEY): My fingers are not on your face. I do not see your face. I have turned your face away. I have turned you away, and you have gone.

SAWNEY:
You did see him then? He said those things? He might have been me. Was it me you saw, Solomon?

SOLOMON:
The face was not clear, it must have been you.

SAWNEY:
If you could be me, would you say those things?

SOLOMON:
I hope so. How could I be you?

JOT:
By thinking about it. If I think: "What would Solomon think, what would Solomon do?" I can be you. That's how Lila knew what Rain would say.

RAIN:
I see. So I could think to myself, how would Lila feel with Sawney's fingers on her face. And then I'd be feeling the fingers, and I would be Lila.

JOT:
That's true.

RAIN:
That's what Sawney says: he often says that. Now you're being Sawney.

LILA:
   If you could be Sawney, what would you do, Jot?

JOT:
   I would eat, I would eat a lot, I would sit here, and chew bones, and suck the juice out, and spit the bad bits away, and do nothing. I wouldn't go out looking and catching food. I wouldn't talk so much, because I'd be eating.

SAWNEY:
   (Laughing largely): Who would catch all this food for you?

JOT:
   You would. I would be Sawney, so you would be Jot. (SAWNEY goes on laughing).

SOLOMON:
   Rain, you be Lila.

RAIN:
   I can't be Lila.

SOLOMON:
   Be Lila loving Sawney You have seen her.

RAIN:
   Yes, but I can't be Lila. You show me.

SOLOMON:
   (Acts this out to SAWNEY's increasing distaste and bewilderment): I put my fingers in my hair and smile. I say "I want a comb, Sawney" and he gives me one, and I comb my hair with it, and he watches me, and I smile like this, and I comb slower and slower, and he loves me, and I put down the comb and I go and stand behind him upon my toes and I put a hand on his neck like this and I whisper into his ear... (whispers something into Sawney's ear. Sawney is still with surprise and then turns round and away from him and looks at him).

RAIN:
(Not alert to what is happening): That was good, Solomon. That was true.

(SOLOMON is as bewildered as SAWNEY and tries to turn the thing off, when he finds he is showing his own response to the emotional situation. He shuts his eyes and leans against the wall, and with his eyes shut speaks).

SOLOMON:
That is what Lila would do.

(Silence).

LILA:
Sawney said I bring him peace, Solomon. But he brings peace to me too. What you did just now is not what he sees. It's what you think he sees. This game doesn't work for you, Solomon, you make lies of it.

SOLOMON:
I felt the game for myself. I was showing you to myself. I made it true. He felt it true. He felt that it was you. And he felt that it was mê too. And that he didn't like. But what he hated was that he felt you through me. Do you know why?

(Silence. LILA does not know why).

SOLOMON:
Because I've changed things.

LILA:
Have you changed things, I don't see what you have changed. Have you changed me? Have you changed Sawney? Or Jot? Or Rain? I see nothing changed.

SOLOMON:
I have changed the spaces in between you. I have changed the space between you and Sawney, and the space between Rain and Jot is changed too. (Smiles with reluctant irony). And I have changed the spaces between those spaces. Between those spaces I have

changed the spaces.

RAIN:
(Lifts her hand) Feel the wind.

LILA:
Solomon, there is a space between you and what you say.

SOLOMON:
Yes, there is, I see it. But it is there. I don't put it there, but it is there. Can you change it, Lila? Can he change it?

LILA:
There is no changing. The spaces are quiet. The sky grows dark, and it grows light again, and dark, and light again. I go to sleep and I wake up. I grow sad, and I grow happy again. My skin grows brown, and then it grows white again. The birds go away and then the birds come back again singing the same songs. There are different birds for different songs, but they never change their songs.

SOLOMON:
Then my song has changed.

LILA:
No, I don't believe you. You have held your song inside you, it has been a secret. Have you not heard it before?

SOLOMON:
Yes. I have heard it. It gave me fear. I spoke about other things. I listened to what I heard from you, and him, and them. You say that nothing changes, but my secret speaks to me of changes. It's not what my eyes see or my ears hear, but what is spoken to me. And there is no space between me and that.

LILA:
You must lose this secret.

SOLOMON:
I cannot.

(Pause).

RAIN:
It's cold tonight. It is cold. (She goes to SOLOMON and looks at him). Come on, it's cold. (She draws him to the fire, making him sit between her and JOT).

SAWNEY:
A secret inside yourself?! A secret. That speaks to you. A secret speaking lies. Lies, lies.

JOT:
(Below the belt). Lies are a pity. A pity for God, and a pity for us.

SAWNEY:
WHO?   Who?   Who.

(SAWNEY grabs a handful of meat from the pot, crushes it in his hand, and stares again at his open hand).

SAWNEY:
Lies are a pity. Who said that? A pity for God. Who said that? A pity for me. Who said that? You said that (shaking his dripping hand at himself). You said it! You were holding a leaf, a leaf, a leaf. You said that. In the night, when my blood mixes with the darkness, is mixed with the darkness, in the night then you say that. That's when you say it, in the dark, when everything is lies. 'Lies are a pity.' A pity for God and a pity for me. In the dark. In the dark you say it. When I sleep you say it. Not when I stand here and know you in my belly, and on my skin, on my hand, not when I feel you in my mouth, and in this throat that speaks to you. Not when the day has been but is not gone. Not when the light still holds the sky above the land. Not when I feel my feet upon the sand, and this hand on the rock, and see, and with my own eyes see my own, my own and lovely faces still with the sun showing them to my eyes. O. (His eyes light on SOLOMON). O Solomon. O my son Solomon, O Solomon, my son, my son! Where have you been in the dark, that it was so dark? Where have you been? How have you let the darkness in, to grow and seek its way

into your heart, into your bone, bone made from my bone, after my bone, heart after my heart? Why does the darkness speak to you with a voice, with a simple voice that you can hear, as if you loved it? O Solomon, O secret Solomon, O Solomon with a secret, O Solomon with black blood, O Solomon with the black voice in your heart, O Solomon you do not hear us when we speak, you do not hear our love... when we speak love you hear the dark gathering in the sea, and the black night coming on the wind, and the secret creature shifting at your back. When we speak love your black love speaks to you and tells you lies. Solomon has killed Solomon. Solomon has taken Solomon into the dark and the dark is a long way for Solomon, a long way for Solomon to go, a long way for Solomon to go... alone. Your night has come, Solomon, your night has come for you. Then go into your long night, go into your long dark home, go where your secret takes you.

RAIN:
Does he want him away?

JOT:
Aye!

RAIN:
Where can he go?

JOT:
Everywhere.

RAIN:
Will he come back?

JOT:
I would.

RAIN:
Will he go? Would you go?

JOT:
No. I would not go. He will go, but I would not. I would wait in the dark behind the fire, and when Solomon and

you, and Lila and Sawney went into the cave to sleep, I would crawl up to the fire and stay there till morning. And when the day came I would go that way up the beach and lie upon that rock and watch. And when the night came I would come to the fire again.

RAIN:
He would know. He would wait for you outside the ring of the fire and catch you by the ankle...

JOT:
And break my neck? Solomon runs faster than Sawney.

SAWNEY:
O Solomon, my son Solomon, I hear the black voice in your heart.

LILA:
Solomon will walk down the edge of the sea listening to the black voice. He will walk with his shadow before him and with his shadow behind him, listening to the black voice. He will hear the call of the birds, and wait till they tell him to come back. He will hear the sea whisper to the sand, and wait till they tell him to come back. He will hear the leaves falling from the trees, and wait till they tell him to come back. But the birds and the sea and the sand and the leaves speak only to each other.

SAWNEY:
O Solomon, my son Solomon.

LILA:
And Solomon will not come back. He will look at the sun day on day on day until his eyes grow white.

JOT:
I will come with you Solomon, we will go into the land. The sea is too far. We will go into the land, and go and go and go until we find a place.

SOLOMON:
I have a place. It is a place with no birds to wail into my ear, no sea to slide about my feet, and no sad

shining sun to want my eyes for his. I have a place which
has no name of Sawney's.

SAWNEY:
O Solomon my son.

SOLOMON:
"O Solomon my son!" That man will catch cold. Put
him to bed. Let him sleep. Let his blood mix with the
darkness and hear the black voice in my heart. "O
Solomon with the black voice in your heart!" I know a
place, it is my own and given secret, and not you or you or
you or (to Rain) even you can come there. This tall man
my father, this namer of names we do not need, this
something walking up and down, this bringer of our
meat, this child of rock and sea and sun, this echo
Sawney holding out my name with tears weeping from
his tongue as if he did me harm and could not help it.
He could not help it! I could not help it. I have spoiled
his place for him. This bit of sea and sand and rock has
black secrets walking in it, and I must walk them out.
Well well well well well. Put him to bed, put all your-
selves to bed. I shall be gone before you wake.

(They exit, he takes no endearments).

My name is Solomon. I am not so simple as I was, so,
I am learning. I like the way (runs his fingers through
the air) my fingers move, I like the way they answer. I
like the way that river runs behind the wood; I do not
like the sea. The sea is heavy. Sea, I leave you. My
name is Solomon, and I shall call my place Solomon.
In it I will sleep the days away, and when the nights come
the moon will be my company and smile at my simplicity
- but I will learn from her. She knows me well. I like
myself. I like that. I like the taste of my own teeth. I
like the taste of my words. I like doing. Now I shall
have doing. I like now. Now it will be always now. Now
I am now. What will I eat? I shall eat silence, the sky,
I shall eat anything. I shall be more than one. I shall
meet myself and not know who I am. I shall spring upon myself from trees and laugh, and not ask why. The
moon will tell me why, in her own time. She knows who
I am. I shall catch minnows with two fingers, and swa-

llow them, and swallows with blue wings and finger
them. I shall spark in the dark until the stars say "Look."
I shall leap into the air... and stay there. I shall let
butterflies dance in my hair, and bang my head on rainbows. I shall be a moment-picking man, a man with sun
and light to live upon. I shall be everywhere where no
one is, and where they are I shall have been and left
my colour. What is my colour? I am not green or black
or yellow or white or blue. I am not red or gold or
orange. What is my colour? I am the colour of the air
above the waves, and birds fly in me, and in my moving shadow fishes swim. I am less simple for each word
I speak. I shall speak words like sands upon the shore;
I shall speak more; there will be more words of me
than sand beside the sea. I shall be all questions, cool
and quick and careless. I shall hang icicles on stars
and climb into the sky, and then let go and down and
down and down until the wind brings me to my place. My
place is here. This is my place. There is a place in me
that's mine but this is where it grew, this is where
Sawney steps onto the ice and wanders like a fir tree
scratching heaven with its frozen hair. This is where
darkness whispers in his ear, and comes in daylight
nudging at his back and makes him question 'Who?'
(mocking) Who? Who? Who? He holds his questions
close... but I have seen them come and go across his
face, and seen him shiver as they twist within his blood
and chew upon the bone which is his pride. Questions are
little things upon the skin; he scratches them until they
swell and lie about his limbs like spiders working at
their webs, quenching all the movement of his hope and
need; all his doing, going, asking grows thick and fat
upon itself until his skill to do to ask is strangled
in its own dumb spit. O Sawney, Sawney's son Sawney,
why do you moan and groan when you say Who? Why not
say Who? A question is a minnow, a moment, a swallow
in the air, it cannot be crushed beneath great Sawney's
feet. A question is a fancy in the air, it cannot be bruised
and harried to its den and killed by rage of asking.
Sawney, Sawney, your questions have no den, come from
no fathering, spring from no coupling in the grass. Questions have no family with each other. I know what questions
are. Questions know Solomon. I will have your questions,
Sawney. Solomon will have Sawney's questions. Sawney

can catch men. Solomon can catch questions. Catch
your men, Sawney. Fill your belly. Empty your
backside upon the ground of men that you have caught
and groan and moan and heave beneath the labour of
your questions. I shall make friends with them, and
they with me. And you will not know Solomon.

(Meanwhile RAIN has arrived but not appeared: she is
standing in the darkness at the back of the aisle or
something).

SOLOMON:
Is Jot not with you?

RAIN:
No.

SOLOMON:
Can you bring him?

RAIN:
He is asleep, and Sawney's hand is on his head.

SOLOMON:
I have shared Sawney's dreams. He has pulled hair of
mine out until I bled, twitching and muttering in his
sleep and dribbling down his chin. How wide a sleep is
Sawney's, to lie on the rock with his arms spread like
branches of a tree, and Lila stuck to the sweaty bark
of his neck, and Jot upon one hand and the other hand
on me.

RAIN:
Why Jot? What do you want with Jot?

SOLOMON:
Oh leave him where he is. He knows things I have not
shared. (Takes her head in his hands) But I have shared
enough.

RAIN:
Will you come back?

SOLOMON:
>You will not have time to wait. When I come back I will be different (this very quietly), you will be different, this place will be different.

RAIN:
>Will I be happy then still? Will I laugh?

SOLOMON:
>What makes you laugh now?

RAIN:
>When something makes me laugh.

SOLOMON:
>When I come back you will laugh at three somethings at the same time, or four or five. Your laughing will be more: it will be three or four or five laughs all mixing.

RAIN:
>Will that be easy?

SOLOMON:
>It's what will happen.

RAIN:
>You're going to hurt Sawney.

SOLOMON:
>No I'm not.

RAIN:
>I know you are.

SOLOMON:
>I will not hurt him. When it is done he will not be hurt.

RAIN:
>What done?

SOLOMON:
>God *Who* God *Who* God *Who*... out *there* when the sea freezes.

RAIN:
> He says God; he says Who. What do you mean?

SOLOMON:
> That is it. Nothing; I mean nothing. But I will before he ever will.

RAIN:
> You will what?

SOLOMON:
> I will know.

RAIN:
> Sawney is not silly, Solomon. He is just not happy.

SOLOMON:
> You always say "happy," as if to be happy was a thing.

RAIN:
> It is a thing. It is a thing in me. It is like you with your secret - laughter is my secret and to me it is no secret. I think your secret is secret to you, you are not easy with it, but I am easy with my laughter. I sit in my laughter like a seaflower in its pool. The pool is cool and still, and flickers ripple on it in the sun, and things happen in my pool and I am happy, but the sun is strong and the wind is loud and the sea floods into my pool and so I am happy, but sometimes I would to lie under the ice while the sea freezes and laugh later.

SOLOMON:
> I would not like to lie under the ice.

RAIN:
> No, Solomon; you are silly.

SOLOMON:
> And Sawney, he is not silly.

RAIN:
> Sawney never looks in pools.

SOLOMON:
    I like pools.

RAIN:
    To look at, but you don't live in one. You live in yourself, although you think you don't. You think you live outside us all, but you don't: you live in yourself and you live in all of us. You like Sawney sending you away, you think you made him do it, but you didn't, he did it because Lila made it happen. You think when Lila combs her hair, she is combing her hair; but when she combs her hair she speaks, it is a voice and Sawney hears it. You like Sawney sending you away, because it makes you strong and alone from us, but you know it is not true: you are not going away, he has not sent you away. You are happy and you pretend not to be: I am happy and I would like not to be.

SOLOMON:
    Happy! God! Combs! Who! Pools! Ice! Laughing flowers! Silly Solomon! Youme you me himher himher who WHO!

RAIN:
    That's not true.

SOLOMON:
    True! I'll true you! I'll God you ! I'll who you! I will show you truth, you will see truth, I'll make you eat truth, I will make truth in this place.

    (Exit SOLOMON).

RAIN:
    Listen to the sea.
    (pause)
    Feel the wind.
    (pause)
    It is cold tonight.
    (longer pause)
    The ice is coming. It will come to my pool. Soon the limpets will drop from the rocks and I will suck them. And the seaweed will be hard, and crackle when I break it. And I will run up the sand and leave no footprints;

until the snow comes, and white everywhere it will be
then, white on the rocks, white on the sand, white on
the cold sea. Snow everywhere. Except in my pool.
When I talk to my pool after the darkness, while the ice
is still on it, my pool will talk to me again. When we
have spoken I will put my finger on it just a little and
then strongly and the ice will break, slowly break, and
slip down and bounce in the water, and then there will
be no answers until another night has been. But I will
see my sea flower riding white in the dark water. So I
will pick all the ice out and she will have the daylight,
poor thing. I will go and see her.

(RAIN goes to her pool and kneels on the edge).

RAIN:
Pool, it is cold now, have you been listening? (Runs
her hand through the water, and jerks it out, it is so
cold). Ho! (a little whoop). Yes, you have! Pool, if I
talk to you will you let the ice come now? It is cold,
you know, it is time for the ice, and my sea flower has
had a long summer. (She blows on the top of the water).
There. Now you are moving. I thought you were asleep.
Waves in the grass make him sad. But not me. (Blows
again). He said the sea was dark and deep, and I said
that's because it has no rest, even when the ice is on
it it has no rest, but my pool rests, don't you, pool?
You and my white sea flower are friends. You be kind
to my white sea flower tonight when the ice comes. You
will let the ice come tonight, won't you, pool? You will
speak to me tonight. I won't ask you too much. I won't
ask you anything. (Leans forward confidentially over her
pool). They're all asking questions. Nothing but questions.
They all want to know things, as if they didn't know
enough, as if they couldn't just wait. If you wait you see
things, but you don't have to see everything. You don't
see everything, sitting here, you and my white sea
flower. You and my white sea flower and me, we don't
see everything. I could empty us all into the sea and we
would see everything... but I won't (hasty reassurance),
I won't do that. Oh, my white sea flower has closed up.
I can just see you there, sea flower. Answer me, pool.
Let the ice come. Answer me, or I will pluck your sea
flower and throw it into the sea. I will pick off the petals

one by one, and crush them, and throw it all, all broken, in the sea. And I will take your ferns, and find your little fishes out, and all your shells and stones and crabs and sea weeds I will have, and put them in the sea... and you will be just water (during this she is getting carried away by destruction... without knowing it, she is needing help from the pool and getting none. Destruction is in the air, and has infected her). And I will fill the water up with sand and sand and sand and sand... and choke you, pool. Choke you. Choke you. Choke you. (Climax. Pause). Oh no. Oh sea flower. Poor thing. Oh my poor pool oh my pretty pool. I will not I will not I will not oh I hope I will not. I hope oh oh oh oh oh oh (pause) ...oh...

ECHO FROM THE POOL:
(This means the ice has formed, and the pool speaks with RAIN's voice) O.

RAIN:
(Trying it out) Oh.

ECHO:
O.

RAIN:
(Happy) Oh.

ECHO:
O.

RAIN:
O pool.

ECHO:
Pool.

RAIN:
Rain.

(No echo).

RAIN:
Rain.

ECHO:
> Rain.

RAIN:
> You have let the ice come.

ECHO:
> Come.

RAIN:
> It will be day soon. Soon the sea will freeze.

ECHO:
> Ease.

RAIN:
> I shall not take your sea flower.

ECHO:
> Hour.

RAIN:
> I shall just speak to you.

ECHO:
> To you.

RAIN:
> And you will say what you want.

ECHO:
> What you want.

RAIN:
> Jot is better than Solomon.

ECHO:
> Better than Solomon.

RAIN:
> Solomon is silly. Silly Solomon.

ECHO:
> Silly Solomon.

RAIN:
>Solomon is the hollow man.

ECHO:
>The hollow man.

RAIN:
>Hollow man Solomon.

>(The echo is silent).

RAIN:
>Hollow man Solomon.

ECHO:
>Sawney fallen.

RAIN:
>Sawney fallen!

ECHO:
>Sawney fallen.

RAIN:
>I don't believe you.

ECHO:
>Leave you.

RAIN:
>I will not leave you.

ECHO:
>I will not leave you.

>(Pause).

RAIN:
>Your answers to my questions are lies.

ECHO:
>(Mocking) Questions are lies.

RAIN:
> No. The answers are lies. They are what you say.

ECHO:
> They are what you say.

RAIN:
> I ask the questions. You answer them.

ECHO:
> You answer them.

RAIN:
> How do I answer? I do the asking.

ECHO:
> The asking.

RAIN:
> I want kind answers.

ECHO:
> (Mocking) Want kind answers.

RAIN:
> Why are you not kind?

ECHO:
> (Indignant) Not kind?

RAIN:
> Yes. Why do you tell lies?

ECHO:
> You tell lies.

RAIN:
> No I don't. I just ask questions. I don't tell you. Find the truth!

ECHO:
> You find the truth.

RAIN:
> I don't know where.

ECHO:
> Nowhere.

RAIN:
> Then why ask me?

ECHO:
> Ask me.

RAIN:
> But why ask you? I don't know what you are, I don't know who...

ECHO:
> Who.

RAIN:
> Who?

ECHO:
> Who.

RAIN:
> That's what Sawney asks.

ECHO:
> Sawney asks.

RAIN:
> Why does he ask that? He knows us all. He should not ask who.

ECHO:
> He should not ask who.

RAIN:
> Who should he ask?

ECHO:
> Ask.

RAIN:
>   You do not tell me. I ask and ask and ask.

ECHO:
>   Ask and ask and ask.

RAIN:
>   Not any more.

ECHO:
>   Why do you weep?

RAIN:
>   I weep for Sawney's sake.

ECHO:
>   I weep for Sawney's sake.
>
>   Scene ends with RAIN weeping. Slow fade.

Scene Two

(In the cave. SAWNEY sleeps with his hand on JOT's head. LILA is sitting up. Meaningless treasure is heaped about them.)

SAWNEY:
(In his sleep, shouts) Lila, Lila. Lila.

LILA:
(Softly to him in his sleep) Yes, Sawney.

SAWNEY:
(In a light happy voice) Sometime we'll make the man again.

(SAWNEY turns over happily, relinquishing his hold on JOT. JOT rolls over on one elbow, and looks at LILA).

JOT:
(Quietly) Where is Rain?

LILA:
At her pool. I think the ice has come. When I was a child there was no ice. It was always hot, and the birds had many colours, so that they shone in the sun. And the flowers, the big flowers, red and heavy some were, others were light as the breeze that swung them on long stems, blue and gold and all the colours of those pretty birds that hid in them when danger stooped. It was always summer then. The beasts were lazy, and walked as if they slept, blinking through sunshot eyes as each foot lent its warm weight to warmer earth. I touched them as they passed and passed my hand along their

yellow fur, and yet they would not stop or care or turn
their heads to see so full of dreams they were, pacing
so slow and silent on their paths through feathered
grass, through poppy-smelling reeds, through hanging
moss borne from the darker branches of great trees
whose highest leaves held creatures darting in the light
so quick in flight they had no other shadow but their
wings, and yet among the leaves were things, squirrels
with long tongues which darted out so quickly from their
mouths that they could catch them. And often when the
bird would fight against his foe, they both would tumble
down and down and down into green gloom where snakes
and serpents, wound with wakeful eyes round clammy
trunks, ended their wrestling fall with easy jaws.

And I, with swarthy skin against the sun, drank from
the milk of coconuts and gourds, and swallowed fruits
as blue and plump as bruises, hanging so thick from
branches burdened to the ground that round their dripping
clusters insects swarmed and hummed leaving the
air the colour of their noise. And in among the smaller
shrubs and vines grew little berries, tart and bitter to
the parching throat, which when I'd slaked my dry
mouth with richer grapes would prick against my teeth
and sting fresh appetite. And sometimes when the sky
grew tired with heat, and weary branches let their ripe
fruit fall, slow thundery raindrops came through the
far-off patterns of the leaves and cooled my ear with
whispers. Then quickly flowers were jewels and moss
was treasure and long laburnum dripped like melting
gold, and in the interstices of the stones small snails
and lizards, spiders and old toads, slid their wet scales
against the cavern walls into the business of the flooded
day. First there was murmur in the tops of trees where
the sky moved to ease the spats of rain, and though you
could not see the branches tossed to lay your hand upon
the unmoved trunk you knew the coming splendour of
the storm, until the burning jungle heaved and bellowed
in its dreams and found the whole world water. Great
rivers grew where little trickles ran, and swans sat on
them, cygnets in their wings, and tall flamingoes beat
against the wind to find a higher perch above the surge.
And round them in the trees were watching eyes, as
little creatures shivered from the rain, and saw their

masters ruffled from their lairs shake angry paws and
pick fastidious ways to proper earth where they could
sit and lord it in their prides, with big unblinking eyes
and swishing tails, letting the storm borrow their wild-
erness and waiting for its idle strength to spend. Which,
when it had, the sun unburst its heat, and drew the water steaming from the ground and with its stupid vapour
hung the air, and everything became itself again. Among
their drying stones the lizards lurked, and from the hill
the lions swung their way, drooping their heads and
blinking in their dreams as if the sky had never touched
their peace. And after they had passed I saw a man, a
figure made of stone who stood where that brief torrent
had splashed down, sudden and strong; thinking I saw
him move I held my breath, but he was stone and still
and blind as silence, and all around him in the working
grass the insects hummed, and birds' wings rushed
again, and all the noises heard themselves once more.

(JOT is deeply moved).

JOT:
That was strange words.

LILA:
They came from a strange place.

JOT:
What place was that?

LILA:
(Sighs a change-of-mood sigh).

JOT:
What place was that?

LILA:
I have forgotten now.

JOT:
It was like birth to me, Lila, like being born among
reasons.

LILA:
> I have forgotten now.

JOT:
> I haven't. I have it all. I'll keep it. I'll wear it, I'll find it, Lila.

LILA:
> This was your place, Jot.

JOT:
> You said 'was'.

LILA:
> Yes.

JOT:
> It's cold here, Lila.

LILA:
> I know.

JOT:
> It's colder than just cold.

> (LILA nods sadly).

JOT:
> The ice is coming. I wish it would not come.

LILA:
> The ice has come. I hear Rain weeping.

JOT:
> I hear it too.

> (There is a pause).

JOT:
> Winter.

LILA:
> Winter.

JOT:
>   Our hearts are broken from our lives. O Lila, Lila, how can we make the sea not freeze? How can we bring back Solomon to the feast? How can we bring back Sawney as he was, and you and he go loving in the sun, and I be simple to myself again, and Rain, poor Rain, not know what weeping is?

LILA:
>   Never. No more.

JOT:
>   When Rain laughed and we said why and she said she'd be frozen in the sea and stand there laughing till the spring and we'd throw snow at her and tease her it was like such a game, the games we do, all the things we do, all the little things we always do, and liking everything, and kindness in between us all the time, and now time's gone cruel and turned us in ourselves and everything is getting lost, and we're all being taken from our place and left with awful empty spaces everywhere and inside here, (pauses) and you say never?

LILA:
>   (After long silence) When you were a child, Jot.

JOT:
>   I am still.

LILA:
>   (Smiles) When you were a little child... do you remember?

JOT:
>   No, I don't (looking at his hands).

LILA:
>   Try. Think backwards.

JOT:
>   Oh well, the swimming.

LILA:
>   What swimming?

JOT:
   Swimming in the sea. I remember that.

LILA:
   What do you remember about it?

JOT:
   I remember when I swam. I remember swimming.

LILA:
   You can't swim.

JOT:
   (Vexed) I did once.

   (A pause).

JOT:
   Once. When I was wee. I swam once.

LILA:
   What was it like?

JOT:
   I don't remember.

LILA:
   Did you like it, or not?

JOT:
   It was cold, no, it was hot.

LILA:
   How far did you swim?

JOT:
   I couldn't see... it was under the water.

LILA:
   Well, how did you breathe?

JOT:
   The same as usual.

LILA:
>Wasn't it wet then?

JOT:
>Of course it was wet. I was under the water.

LILA:
>Tell me what it was like.

JOT:
>There were no flowers. There were no birds. There was no grass or sky or wind. There were no colours and no words, no trees and no creatures. I swam once, you see. I didn't like it. So I swam once.

LILA:
>What else can you remember?

JOT:
>Can't you see?

LILA:
>You're not going to remember.

JOT:
>What do you remember for? Why do you always remember? Why do you always remember at me?

LILA:
>Remembering is a way to be sure.

JOT:
>(Getting excited) How do we be sure now? With him! ... (He stabs his finger behind him at SAWNEY and we see that SAWNEY's eyes are wide open and he is lying on his back staring upwards at the roof of the cave)... With him, swimming head first into all the things that have nothing to do with us... floating in darkness and calling it his blood and saying how terrible that is... You know I heard a man say to him... this: 'The best pleasure is to stand high on the ground of truth and to see the errors and wanderings and mists and tempests beneath.' Mmm. There! And do you know what Sawney

said? Do you know what he talked about? I'll tell you. A
fish. And this is what he said about this fish: 'Under the
ice he listens, deep down, far down, under the white ice,
in the dark, where the water moves he is listening when
I talk. He is moving where I move, under me, under my
feet, far down, deep down, when I move moving with me,
listening.' (JOT has chanted this with all the relish of an
Anglican priest). Well... that's what fishes do. What
does he expect a fish to do, stand on a hillside and look
what's happening below? That's what he's supposed to
do! Do you know what he's doing? He's living on top of
the ground and wanting to live underneath it. Or to live
everywhere at once for all I know. He lives on the edge
of the sea so he wants to know what's going on there
too. He wants to swim in the ground and walk on the bottom of the sea. He wants too much, Lila! But still he
doesn't know what it is he wants. And he never will. The
day before yesterday I would have helped him, I would
have joined him, but I can't now, he wouldn't see I was
there. He has found new hungers. His tongue wants new
tastes. And there is no meat for them. He will have to
eat the whole world.

(Enter RAIN).

RAIN:
It's morning.

(JOT and LILA look at her, they have nothing left to say,
and RAIN feels suddenly at a loss).

RAIN:
It's morning.

SAWNEY:
(Flat) It is morning and the ice has come.

RAIN:
Yes. It has.

SAWNEY:
I heard it. Have you been to your pool?

RAIN:
    (Going to him): Yes I have. It was weeping.

SAWNEY:
    (Holding out a hand for her to take): Weeping passes. We do things and weeping passes. We will do things today.

RAIN:
    What things shall we do?

SAWNEY:
    Now Rain I called you, for I like rain, but there was a moment I nearly called you by another name.

RAIN:
    Let me guess! Foam?

SAWNEY:
    No no no.

RAIN:
    Leaf?

SAWNEY:
    No.

RAIN:
    I know; Fire!

SAWNEY:
    I nearly named you Fire, because you always liked the fire. And today, how would you like to see the biggest fire you ever saw? A fire as tall as me and as deep as Lila? That's what I shall make for you. That's what we shall do. Hey Lila?

RAIN:
    Why are you both so quiet?

        Slow fade into darkness.

Scene Three

(In this scene SOLOMON, on the one hand, and in the wood, is digging a pit which will be a trap, and SAWNEY on the other hand and on the shore with RAIN as his apprentice is collecting wood which will be heaped on a large sled and dragged by him out onto the ice. You will have to use light on the party to which the text gives speech and action, and this will be turnabout. The two separate activities should respond to each other by some clear element of ritual or mime or pace. SOLOMON is back in ordinary clothes and so is everyone else by this time. Mark that the air is cold cold cold).

(Light on SOLOMON)

SOLOMON:
(Digging slowly and rhythmically to the time of the verse)
There was a man of double deed
Sowed his garden full of seed.
When the seed began to grow
It was a garden full of snow.
When the snow began to crack
It was a stick across my back.
When my back began to smart
It was a black knife in my heart.
When my heart began to bleed
Then death and death and death indeed.

(He is already a long way down in this deep pit he is digging).

That's a long way up there; a man could live down here if he wanted to be with the moles, or if he had nothing to do, if he wanted just to sit and whistle and pass worms

through his fingers. Digging is quite a thing to do; I like
it. Good smell down here, the earth smells good and wet,
very soft, too soft, yes, will need to throw some big
stones down in here when I've done. Give my trap some
teeth, break some bones on them, no jumping out again.
I am making jaws for darkness, a throat for the night,
a belly for death.

(Fade off SOLOMON, lights up on SAWNEY and RAIN. Both
empty armfuls of wood onto imaginary pile).

RAIN:
Will it last all day?

SAWNEY:
No, it will last all night. All night you will see it burning there.

RAIN:
Where? Burning where?

SAWNEY:
Where fire has never burnt, where burning's never been.
Where the ice will cook and crack and the sea will curdle,
and through the smoke in the water the fish will come, as
I would if the sun came down and sat upon the shore.

RAIN:
The sea the sea. You're going to set fire to the sea. Oh
how beautiful. It will shine all the way along the ice to
me. And before that I will see you take a brand from the
fire at the cave, and I will see it move across the ice
long after you are out of sight, and then - oh! - it will
shine up into the darkness and splash the stars and blaze
and be beautiful. And I will be warm just standing here.
(Pause). What will happen when the fire dies.

SAWNEY:
(Very slow and heavy): When the fire dies the fish will
come. The fish will come.

(Fade off SAWNEY and RAIN, lights up on SOLOMON. His
pit is finished, he is sitting on its floor, making muddy
lines on his face.

SOLOMON:
When the night is dark he will come. His feet will know no difference in the grass. I will twine roots and branches and cover them with turf and leaves until the ground is as it was. And he will come light-footing along (mimes) sniffing the night in the air, muttering his memories in his mouth, his eyes as big as eggs polished by the moon and so - the earth will make a little shiver, and he will stop, and the ground will bend, and he will KNOW and as he knows he will be gone, holding onto the air with his arms, kicking out with his legs shouting and staring and falling and hooof... onto my stones, my big rocks, my sharp little ones, my bone-breakers. And then I will let him lie there a little (pats the ground), until he has thought of something to say, and I will look down from that branch, with just my eyes over the edge, and I will see him in the moonlight and he will see me. And he will say "Oh Solomon", and I will say nothing, and he will be down here, and I will be up there, and he will know I am someone but perhaps not me after all, and I shall say nothing and lay my head on the bough and count the stars, and after a long while he will think I have gone away, and when I know he is thinking that, softly, very softly, I will say 'Oh Sawney' in this voice (uses a different voice) and he will wonder, and he will say 'Who? Who is there?' And I shall say nothing and count more stars, and he will say 'Who?' for quite a long time, he always does, and he will talk to Who, and I will listen, and he will ask Who questions, this question and that question and all his questions, and the pit will stink with questions, he will choke in questions. But I shall not, I shall hear them one at a time, and I shall know his questions, his questions that run so thick in him. I shall go now, and pour down my stones, my bonnie bone-breakers.

(Slow fade off Solomon).

(We return to SAWNEY and RAIN. SAWNEY is in great humour).

SAWNEY:
After tonight, anything!

RAIN:
    Anything at all!

SAWNEY:
    Anything, everything, anything!

RAIN:
    New things!

SAWNEY:
    Oh new things! Things we don't know!

RAIN:
    Things to laugh for!

SAWNEY:
    You'll laugh for ever!

RAIN:
    You'll laugh for ever!

SAWNEY:
    We'll all laugh for ever! Everything will laugh for ever!

RAIN:
    Ever and ever and ever and ever...

SAWNEY:
    ... ... ever and ever and ever and ever!

RAIN:
    Unless we don't want to.

SAWNEY:
    Don't want to?

RAIN:
    Well not all the time.

SAWNEY:
    Why not?

RAIN:
    Well you can get tired   laughing.

SAWNEY:
>Not this laughing you can't. Are you tired now?

RAIN:
>No.

SAWNEY:
>Well then, this is what it will be like.

RAIN:
>Anything after tonight.

SAWNEY:
>Everything, anything, everything!

RAIN:
>Anything at all!

SAWNEY:
>Everything at all always!

RAIN:
>Always and always and always and ever and ever and ever!

SAWNEY:
>Laughing for ever!

RAIN:
>All of us laughing and laughing and laughing!

SAWNEY:
>(Joke): When we want to!

RAIN:
>(Laughing like anything): When we want to!

SAWNEY:
>When we want to!

RAIN:
>When it's like now!

SAWNEY:
> When everything's like everything!

RAIN:
> (They are quiet again). Oh I hope it comes!

(Fade off SAWNEY and RAIN).

(Light on SOLOMON).

SOLOMON:
> What will it be like after? What will I be like? He will last a long while. It will be a long meal, so I will put him down in salt, the biggest bits. First I shall have the heart and then the liver. What will they taste of? Will they taste different? Where will the questions be? He thinks they are in his blood. I think they are in the bone, juicy in the marrow, questions to suck and pry out with my tongue. And then what will it be like with me, with him in me, and me him walking, thumping on trees, bruising the clouds with my head, holding the wind in my fist, moving across the land, away from here, taking my Lila with me with his hunger and with mine, moving across the land. What will it be like there, where they came from, the ones we have eaten, what will it be like where they live, and what will Solomon and Sawney not do there? Oh Sawney Sawney you will come to your might in me, not sitting around here asking, wondering, fearing, and in your idle time finding combs along the shore and playing with little pleasures, dancing your little dances round mere food, making a fancy feast of little eating, making a song and dance about your being as if the days were long for you to cast away like pebbles in the sea.

(Fade off SOLOMON who now leaves the stage).

(Before the lights go up, LILA, JOT and RAIN are holding hands in a ring round SAWNEY and moving round him. He is being the fire (which he is going to light later on the ice) and they are celebrating him. From the dark we hear the voice of SAWNEY and the lights fade up slowly while he speaks).

SAWNEY:
> I am the fire.

LILA: JOT: RAIN:
> (simultaneously) The fire that calls the fish.

SAWNEY:
> I call the fish, I call the monster of the sea.

OTHERS:
> He is the fire.

SAWNEY:
> I call the swift sea-monster.

OTHERS:
> He burns upon the sea.

SAWNEY:
> I will wake the monster.

OTHERS:
> In the far green deep.

SAWNEY:
> I will burn upon the ice.

OTHERS:
> It will awake and move.

SAWNEY:
> The sea will divide before it.

OTHERS:
> It will fly towards the light.

SAWNEY:
> Like a shadow towards the sun.
>
> (LILA, JOT and RAIN sit down round him, no longer holding hands).
>
> I shall be the sun, I shall burn upon the ice and the

monster will come to me, fast from the far green deep, swifter than stars fall, a voice, a voice calling through the water, voice of the sea-deep, voice of the hiding darkness, tongue of the black silence, tongue of the unheard sea-deep, called from the sea-sleep, voice sent in answer, voice come to my voice, echo to my asking, dark voice waking long silent to my sounding, long-waited waiting one, waking to my asking, forth from the sea-deep coming to the sea-flame coming to my fingertips, rising through the water, riding on the sea-glow, called to the sea-feast, fire through the water, taker of the sea-gift, taker of the sea-bride, deep dark hungry one, long-waited hungry one, love-seeking hungry one, fellow-flesh to Sawney.

(SAWNEY, who has worked into an exultation, rushes out pulling LILA by the hand).
(Classical Greek tragic style: strophe and antistrophe).

JOT:
That was not good to hear.

RAIN:
He spoke high words.

JOT:
I fear what he is going to do.

RAIN:
He does not fear the sea-beast.

JOT:
I do not like the rising of his mind.

RAIN:
His thoughts are wild and puzzling.

JOT:
I do not like the look behind his eyes.

RAIN:
He sees a hidden outcome.

JOT:
>He has some deathly purpose.

RAIN:
>He will destroy the monster.

JOT:
>He means some other death.

RAIN:
>Death.

JOT:
>Death nearer to our being.

RAIN:
>Who will be the sea-bride?

JOT:
>One who is worth giving.

RAIN:
>Who will be the sea-lure?

JOT:
>Sawney's precious gift-thing.

RAIN:
>His heart is moving from us.

JOT:
>He gives it to the questions.

RAIN:
>Tongue within the sea-deep.

JOT:
>Dark voice in the sea-glow.

RAIN:
>Asking come in answer.

JOT:
>Coming to meet Sawney.

RAIN:
> Sawney with the sea-gift.

JOT:
> Gift not his for giving.

RAIN:
> Sawney with the sea-bride.

JOT:
> Bride to give the monster.

RAIN:
> Sawney with the cold heart.

JOT:
> Sawney with the cunning eye.

RAIN:
> Sawney with the clever hand.

JOT:
> Sawney not what Sawney is.

> (Pause. The next line RAIN becomes naturalistic again ... a whisper).

RAIN:
> Sawney Sawney Sawney fallen.

JOT:
> (Naturalistic also) Rain, he will take Lila. We must stop them.

RAIN:
> He will not have to take her. She will go.

JOT:
> Rain, I cannot move. I cannot move.

RAIN:
> (Starts to weep) I know, I know.

JOT:
> She will not go, she will not.

RAIN:
> He will go and make his fire upon the ice. And she will follow.

JOT:
> Oh Rain, I cannot move.

SAWNEY:
> (Offstage, on the ice, shouts) Lila! Lila!

JOT:
> (Looks towards the voice) He is not there! He is on the ice. He has gone!
>
> (JOT takes a few steps forward, falls on his knees. plunges his hands into the sand, holds onto it as though the world is falling apart).

JOT:
> Everything is moving. Everything is falling. We are too small for all the size of things!
>
> (Enter SOLOMON).

SOLOMON:
> There is a fire out on the ice.
>
> (Black out).

ACT THREE

(Out on the ice. It is dark. Enter SOLOMON, to be followed shortly by SAWNEY in pursuit through the darkness. The fire, which has not burnt out, can be taken to be behind the seats to the north of the stage, about a furlong distant: the shore being the rest of the mile to the south of the stage. SOLOMON, half-seen in the dark and the smoke, has been teasing SAWNEY, making him unsure who or what it is that has drawn him away from the fire).

SOLOMON:
(Laughing). He is still at it. Chasing unseen figures in the dark. (To SAWNEY, offstage, calls) Hullo! Hullo, old heap of bones! Come here and be welcomed!

(SAWNEY bursts in).

SAWNEY:
Welcomed? Who's there? Solomon? Why welcomed?

(SOLOMON is careful throughout this scene not to get in arms' reach of SAWNEY. With every phrase he speaks he moves, not a boxer's jive, but like a dance with a set distance between the partners, a conspirator's dance melting into shadows).

SOLOMON:
Would Solomon not welcome Sawney?

SAWNEY:
He should, so he should. But here? Why here?

SOLOMON:
Because Solomon lives here.

SAWNEY:
You live here!

SOLOMON:
Aye, I live here.

SAWNEY:
You live here?

SOLOMON:
This is the ice. This is my place.

SAWNEY:
(Laughs unbelieving and ironic). Ho ho ho.

SOLOMON:
(Not joining in) Old old man, you have burnt a hole in my floor.

SAWNEY:
I have...

SOLOMON:
... Aye. Burnt a hole. In my floor. You have let the water in.

SAWNEY:
I have let the monster out.

SOLOMON:
Monster, monster, monster then? I have not seen him.

SAWNEY:
He would not look for you.

SOLOMON:
(Quick as a rat) Who would he look for?

SAWNEY:
(Cagey, strokes his cheek with four fingers) Who would he look for?

SOLOMON:
    Not for you. Your bones are too tough.

SAWNEY:
    What do you know about my bones?

SOLOMON:
    Not so much as I will.

SAWNEY:
    Be still. I want to talk to you. I want to whisper... so that the monster cannot hear. (He makes towards SOLOMON. SOLOMON dances away).

SOLOMON:
    The monster hears everything anyway.

SAWNEY:
    How do you know?

SOLOMON:
    I live here. I know the secret places.

SAWNEY:
    Be still! Let me touch you!

SOLOMON:
    (Almost simultaneously) I have lain there and whispered to him.

    (SAWNEY stops, poised, with his hands out).

SOLOMON:
    Oh yes, we have whispered together.

SAWNEY:
    Lies, lies, lies, lies, lies.

SOLOMON:
    No.

SAWNEY:
    Lies.

SOLOMON:
   Yes.

SAWNEY:
   Be still!

(SOLOMON is standing absolutely still).

SAWNEY:
   Be still!

SOLOMON:
   Sawney...

SAWNEY:
   (Just about to lay his hands on SOLOMON) Yes?

SOLOMON:
   Where is Lila?

(SAWNEY is stopped again, and recoils).

SAWNEY:
   (Statement) Where is Lila. Where I left her.

SOLOMON:
   Alone?

(SAWNEY turns to go, remembering everything).

SOLOMON:
   (Softly) Sawney... <u>Who</u>?

SAWNEY:
   (Punch-drunk) Who?

SOLOMON:
   Who do you think lives...? (Drops a forefinger to point downwards under the ice).

SAWNEY:
   Ah, you do not know.

SOLOMON:
> A one-eyed shark, Sawney. Old, Sawney, with no teeth left. And a shrivelled tail. He lives in the shallows, Sawney, he lives by the shore, he is frightened of the deep. He lives on jellyfish and seaweed, Sawney. I have cracked mussels open for him. He needs soft food. He has a pleading eye, and when I feed him he bends his head as if his life was kind again. A poor old shark, Sawney, with one dim eye. He's not a terror, Sawney, not a voice in the dark, not a wonder, not an enemy, not a secret, not an answer, not a question. But he is hungry, Sawney, hungry for his soft food.

LILA:
> (Offstage, to the north, behind audience, screams: and this would come best taped and through a speaker) Sawney!

SAWNEY:
> (To SOLOMON) You lied. (Shouts) Lila!

LILA:
> Oh Sawney! The beautiful fish!

SAWNEY:
> (To SOLOMON) You lied. (Shouts) Lila! Here! I'm here!

LILA:
> I cannot move, Sawney. Oh Sawney, the beautiful colours!

SAWNEY:
> (To SOLOMON) You lied, you lied. Go from me!

SOLOMON:
> Go to her.

SAWNEY:
> I cannot move. I cannot look there. Lila!

LILA:
> O fine, O beautiful, O depthless eyes!

SAWNEY:
> (Collapsing, nearly weeping) You lied, you lied.

SOLOMON:
> We both lied. You and I.

SAWNEY, LILA:
> O fair, O bright, O subtle circle. O kind caressing one.

SAWNEY:
> (Moaning and weeping) Lila, Lila, no, no.

SOLOMON:
> (Coldly) Listen.

LILA:
> O do not go... Good mystery, kind sudden creature, do not go. (Pause). O do not turn away into the deep. ...Ah! Can I go with you? Oh I fear the deep. O do not go. O do not. Oh, then I will follow. Oh I fear the sea. ... Yes, if you wish it so, yes, yes.
>
> (Long stretching silence).

SAWNEY:
> No, no, no, no. You lied.
>
> (Pause).

SOLOMON:
> You lied.

SAWNEY:
> You lied.'

SOLOMON:
> Of course I lied, but so did she. That was no bright essential from the sky making its glory eager in the sea until she died of strangeness. It was the dying fish, begging for its dinner.

SAWNEY:
> No no, she would not.

SOLOMON:
> Why not? You wanted it.

SAWNEY:
> She did not know.

SOLOMON:
> You wanted it. I knew. So she knew.

SAWNEY:
> It was not to be this, it was not this I wanted.

SOLOMON:
> What, what did you want?

SAWNEY:
> I wanted...

SOLOMON:
> Wanted what?

SAWNEY:
> I wanted...

SOLOMON:
> Wanted who?

SAWNEY:
> I wanted... something. I did not want something! I did not! I did not want wanting. Wanting is here! (Grabs at the dark) And here! And here. You do not know it. But I know it. It was to be a glory. A great burning brightness. It was to be... oh! but the stars could tell you. I would not send my Lila down that sea for little things. You do not know how I have loved her. You do not know how we have loved. Until the waves upon the shore were not enough to match the heart-beats of our love. Until the days and days and days in which we lived were brighter than the sun, and shone, and shone. And I have sent my Lila down the sea because she knew the cruelty of the dark, she knew the great black space behind the sun, she knew the kindness of the light bright day and heard the echo of the breaking night.

SOLOMON:
> She knows more now.

SAWNEY:
Oh go away! What do you do? What have you done? What do you know? What can you say? What can you do?

SOLOMON:
Less than this maybe (gesturing to the north), but it is time for you to know what I can do. Your stomach will not like it, Sawney, when you see. When you have finished, here, come to your hunting-patch Sawney, and see how Solomon does catch his meat.

SAWNEY:
I smell no meat up there tonight.

SOLOMON:
I do Sawney, I smell meat.

SAWNEY:
How can you get meat? You don't know what to say.

SOLOMON:
I will when the time comes, and it will not be long.

SAWNEY:
Oh go away! I must be here alone.

SOLOMON:
Come to your wood Sawney. Come to your hunting-patch. The air is warmer there, the wood is friendly to us, and then besides, I have appetite.

(Exit SOLOMON, to the south).

SAWNEY:
Oh Lila, Lila! Where have you gone and left me here?

(Slow fade).
(Utter blackness. Fifteen seconds).

VOICE OF SAWNEY:
(From the dark, now in the wood) Days and nights, days and nights, where is the boy? Catch meat, catch men, that loon. He wanted Lila. I knew. I knew that. Not now. She's gone now. Where is he? Yes, she's gone now, down

the sea, down the dark, down, down down, hoo-hoof
down there, gone down, gone always, left me always,
left me, Lila left me, poor Sawney, poor Sawney Bean,
poor thing. Well then, now then, no meat, no meat here;
where is the boy? Solomon? Solomon! Not here? Not yet.
Lies, lies, all lies, he wanted Lila, I knew, she knew, she
went away, now I'm all alone, poor Sawney Bean. Whisht!
What's that? Is that you, Sawney? Is that you, Sawney
Bean? Oh I know you. I know you now. In the dark behind
me, in front of me, up and down and all around, Sawney
Bean, poor Sawney Bean, Lila's gone, Sawney, down the
dark sea, nights and days, nights and nights and nights,
that's what we live in now, Sawney, in the dark, in the
night, you and me, no one else, no help, all alone, Sawney
Bean, you and me, no questions, not worth it, no wanting,
not wanted, no asking, no one to ask, only you, you and me,
Sawney Bean. Hey, hey, who's that? What's that, Sawney?
What's that smell? (Pause). I smell... Solomon!

(Through the word 'Solomon' SAWNEY falls down the pit,
which is a long long way. He lands on SOLOMON's bone-
breaking stones, and is mortally damaged. As this happens,
with SAWNEY groaning... after a pause... the lights come
up to a very dim blue. We see SAWNEY spread out, on
his back, all collapsed SOLOMON's voice will come from
above, over the edge of the pit, therefore presumably
taped).

SAWNEY:
(By this time, and after this fall, his wits and his whole
frame are reduced to fumbling; he speaks therefore with
a simpleness falling short of the idiotic). So there's the
moon. (Groans). (Tentatively... an enquiry...). Sawney?
Sawney? Yes, yes. (Groans). O yes. (Pause). Not good.
Oh. (Pause). I have broken my bits. (Pause). Not good.
Oh. (Pause). I have broken my bits. (Pause). All my bits
are broken. Sawney's broken. You are broken, Sawney.
An end, then. (Pause). Then an end. (Pause). (He notices
the stones with his hands). Stones. Rocks. Stones and
rocks. Rocks and stones waiting for Sawney. (Pause). In
the beginning. (Pause). In the beginning I. (Pause). In
the beginning I danced with rocks. I think I did. I did. In
the beginning the air was white, I can't remember, I
drank it then... did I? Well, (pauses) Moon. (Pause).

Nothing. (Pause). I mean you no harm. (Pause. Groans).
I mean you no harm. I mean no harm. I mean nothing.
(Pause.) I mean nothing. Sawney's end. This is Sawney's
end. (Pause). What was it I used to say? Wh..? Wh..?
Whoo? That was it. Whoo? I wonder what that was about.
(Pause. Groans). Well, then, I have broken my bits.
Ooooh-ooh, my blood, my blood is getting out. There,
then, I knew it did. It thinks I'm asleep. I shall see where
it goes. (Pause). Ah, there's a rainbow. And there's
another. No. Not rainbows. (Pause). No, they've gone.
That was good. I liked that. (Groans). (Suddenly coherent).
I think that at the midday I will watch the sun wading in the
water. (Screams). Something might have come! For what
I did... something might have come! Nothing! Nothing
come. Nothing nothing nothing nothing nothing.

SOLOMON's VOICE:
Sawney. Sawney Bean down there. Sawney Bean.

SAWNEY:
Nothing. (Conversationally, to himself) My blood is
getting out.

SOLOMON:
Where are you now, Sawney Bean?

SAWNEY:
(To himself). I think I am asleep. (Groans). Something
might have come. I wanted something true.

SOLOMON:
(Moved) O Sawney, Sawney.

SAWNEY:
I wanted. Something might have come.

SOLOMON:
(Louder). Sawney. Sawney.

SAWNEY:
There's a voice. My blood is getting out.

SOLOMON:
(Louder again). Sawney. Sawney.

SAWNEY:
> There's a voice. Oh oh oh, I have broken all my bits. That was a voice. (Pause). Something might have come. (Dies).

SOLOMON:
> Sawney's not here. I have made Sawney's end. Sawney's dead and I will cover up the blood and bones and stones. And leave this place, and go and sorrow for myself, alone. How could his kindness be so cruel to Sawney Bean. I leave you be. Kind Sawney Bean.

> (Black out).

EPILOGUE.

(Sunlight. JOT is building a little cairn of white pebbles. Enter RAIN carrying more pebbles, which she puts down beside him.)

RAIN:
> What are they for?

JOT:
> To remember.

RAIN:
> Remember what?

JOT:
> Where Sawney sat.

RAIN
> But why, Jot?

JOT:
> So that we shan't sit there.

RAIN:
> (Cheerfully throwing a pebble up and catching it): Will we be here?

JOT:
> Sometime. We might not remember. (Laughs). He would

have liked bigger stones.

RAIN:
    Well let's get him bigger stones.

JOT:
    Big enough for him? We couldn't carry them, Rain. I like these little stones, they're the same size as words.

RAIN:
    It's going to take a lot of them.

JOT:
    That's all right. There's no hurry. Anyway, it's not going to be very big. It's not important, it's just a thing I want to do.

RAIN:
    How slow the sea stands. Time seems to take more time to pass.

    (JOT sits quite still for a long moment).

RAIN:
    Jot?

JOT:
    Listen! How quiet time passes. Time was too loud for Sawney.

    (Fade).

THE END

C AND B PLAYSCRIPTS

* PS 1 TOM PAINE
        by Paul Foster   *21s + 6s6d

* PS 2 BALLS and other plays
        (The Recluse, Hurrah for the Bridge,
        The Hessian Corporal)
        by Paul Foster   *25s + 7s6d

  PS 3 THREE PLAYS
        (Lunchtime Concert, Coda,
        The Inhabitants)
        by Olwen Wymark   *21s + 6s6d

* PS 4 CLEARWAY
        by Vivienne C. Welburn   *21s + 6s6d

* PS 5 JOHNNY SO LONG and
        THE DRAG
        by Vivienne C. Welburn   *25s + 8s6d

* PS 6 SAINT HONEY and
        OH DAVID, ARE YOU THERE?
        by Paul Ritchie   *25s +10s6d

  PS 7 WHY BOURNEMOUTH? and other plays
        (The Missing Links,
        An Apple a Day)
        by John Antrobus   *25s +10s0d

* PS 8 THE CARD INDEX and other plays
        (The Interrupted Act,
        Gone Out)
        by Tadeusz Rozewicz
        trans. Adam Czerniawski   *25s +10s6d

  PS 9 US
        by Peter Brook and others   *42s +21s0d

* PS 10 SILENCE and THE LIE
        by Nathalie Sarraute
        trans. Maria Jolas   *25s + 9s0d

*	PS 11	THE WITNESSES and other plays (The Laocoon Group, The Funny Old Man) by Tadeusz Rosewicz trans. Adam Czerniawski	*25s + 9s0d
*	PS 12	THE CENCI by Antonin Artaud trans. Simon Watson-Taylor	*18s + 7s6d
*	PS 13	PRINCESS IVONA by Witold Gombrowicz trans. Krystyna Griffith-Jones and Catherine Robins	*21s + 8s6d
*	PS 14	WIND IN THE BRANCHES OF THE SASSAFRAS by Rene de Obaldia trans. Joseph Foster	*25s + 9s0d
*	PS 15	INSIDE OUT and other plays (Talking of Michaelangelo, Still Fires, Rolley's Grave, Come Tomorrow) by Jan Quackenbush	*21s + 8s6d
*	PS 16	THE SWALLOWS by Roland Dubillard trans. Barbara Wright	*25s + 9s0d
	PS 17	THE DUST OF SUNS by Raymond Roussel trans. Lane Dunlop	*25s + 9s0d
	PS 18	EARLY MORNING by Edward Bond	*25s + 8s6d
	PS 19	THE HYPOCRITE by Robert McLellan	*25s + 9s0d
	PS 20	THE BALACHITES and THE STRANGE CASE OF MARTIN RICHTER by Stanley Eveling	*30s +12s0d

	PS 21	A SEASON IN THE CONGO by Aime Cesaire	*25s + 9s0d
	PS 22	TRIXIE AND BABA by John Antrobus	*21s + 8s6d
	PS 23	SPRING AWAKENING by Frank Wedekind trans. Tom Osborn	*25s + 9s0d
	PS 24	PRECIOUS MOMENTS FROM THE FAMILY ALBUM TO PROVIDE YOU WITH COMFORT IN THE LONG YEARS TO COME by Naftali Yavin	*25s + 9s0d
*	PS 25	DESIRE CAUGHT BY THE TAIL by Pablo Picasso trans. Roland Penrose	*18s + 8s0d
*	PS 26	THE BREASTS OF TIRESIAS by Guillaume Apollinaire	*18s + 8s0d
	PS 27	ANNA LUSE and other plays (Jens, Purity) by David Mowat	*30s +15s0d
*	PS 28	O and other plays by Sandro Key-Aarberg	*25s + 9s0d
*	PS 29	WELCOME TO DALLAS, MR KENNEDY by Kaj Himmelstrup	*25s + 9s0d
	PS 30	THE LUNATIC, THE SECRET SPORTSMAN AND THE WOMEN NEXT DOOR and VIBRATIONS by Stanley Eveling	*25s +11s0d
*	PS 31	STRINDBERG by Colin Wilson	*21s + 9s0d

* PS 32   THE FOUR LITTLE GIRLS
           by Pablo Picasso
           trans. Roland Penrose   *25s + 9s0d

  PS 33   MACRUNE'S GUEVARA
           by John Spurling   *25s + 9s0d

* PS 34   THE MARRIAGE
           by Witold Gombrowicz
           trans. Louis Iribarne   *25s + 9s0d

* PS 35   BLACK OPERA and
           THE GIRL WHO BARKS LIKE A DOG
           by Gabriel Cousin
           trans. Irving F. Lycett   *25s + 9s0d

* PS 36   SAWNEY BEAN
           by Robert Nye and Bill Watson   *25s + 9s0d

  PS 37   COME AND BE KILLED and
           DEAR JANET ROSENBERG, DEAR
           MRS. KOONING
           by Stanley Eveling   *25s + 9s0d

  PS 38   VIETNAM DISCOURSE
           by Peter Weiss
           trans. Geoffrey Skelton   *25s + 9s0d

* PS 39   HEIMSKRINGLA or
           THE STONED ANGELS
           Paul Foster   *25s + 9s0d

  PS 40   JAN PALACH
           by Alan Burns   *25s + 9s0d

* PS 41   HOUSE OF BONES
           by Roland Dubillard   *25s + 9s0d

* All plays marked thus are represented for dramatic presentation by:
C and B (Theatre) Ltd, 18 Brewer Street, London W1